The Ultimate 401(k) Guide

Eric F. Hogarth, CFP®

Table of Contents

Regulatory Issues

Notes to Readers

This publication contains the opinions and ideas of its author. The strategies outlined in this book may not be suitable for every individual and are not guaranteed or warranted to produce any particular results.

Presentation of performance data herein does not imply that similar results will be achieved in the future. Any such data are provided merely for illustrative and discussion purposes; rather than focusing on the time periods used or the results derived. The reader should instead focus on the underlying principles.

This book is sold with the understanding that neither publisher nor author, through this book, is engaged in rendering legal, tax, investment, insurance, financial, accounting or other professional advice or services. If the reader requires such advice or services, a competent professional should be consulted. Relevant laws vary from state to state.

No warranty is made with respect to the accuracy or the completeness of the information contained herein, and both the author and the publisher specifically disclaim responsibility for any liability, loss, or risk, personal or otherwise, that is incurred as a consequence, directly or indirectly, of the use and application of any of the contents of this book.

Lastly, this book is written under the right of the First Amendment to the Constitution of the United States. This book is written as an outside business activity from my investment advisory and securities business.

The ideas expressed are not meant to be taken as advice that you can act upon.

You should find an individual advisor that you trust to implement these ideas after determining if they are appropriate and suitable for your unique situation.

Introduction

"You are never too old to set another goal or dream a new dream."

C.S. Lewis

As a Financial Advisor with over fifteen years of industry experience, I have had the opportunity to meet with hundreds of people as they approach their retirement. The first emotion many people feel when thinking about their retirement is *fear; not of retiring, but of uncertainty*. The question I most often hear is: ***Am I going to have enough money for the rest of my life?***

The most widely-held investment in the United States is the employer-sponsored plan, typically in the form of the 401(k). Americans save into it diligently for decades, yet as they approach their retirement, most people are not aware of the many options available to them both *before* and *after* retirement, nor the "dangers" that exist in just staying the course.

The goal of this book is to guide you through the many options you have with your 401(k) and to provide you with the clarity you need to make the important decisions that will provide the foundation of your family's financial future.

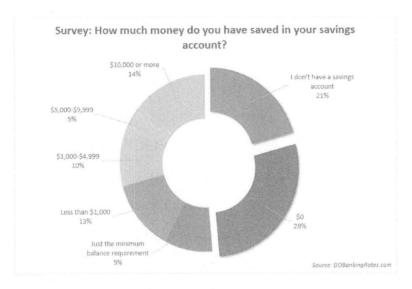

Survey: How much money do you have saved in your savings account?

$10,000 or more 14%

I don't have a savings account 21%

$5,000-$9,999 5%

$1,000-$4,999 10%

Less than $1,000 13%

$0 28%

Just the minimum balance requirement 9%

Source: GOBankingRates.com

(1)

It's taken years and years of good financial decisions and a concrete savings plan to put people in the position they're in today; a position where retirement is no longer a hope, but a reality. Mistakes made close to or in early retirement can put all of that hard-earned savings at risk of running out. As people begin to think about their retirement, they should also be taking a closer look at their often over-looked 401(k) plan and the power it holds for their financial future.

One of the most common questions I get as a
CERTIFIED FINANCIAL PLANNER™ is in regards to
what investors should do with their 401(k) assets. The
term 401(k) references, in particular, an employer-
sponsored retirement plan provided by a for-profit
company. If you are a teacher or a nurse, or someone
working for a nonprofit, then you would most likely
have a 403(b). Or, if you work for a municipality or
perhaps your state, you most likely have a plan in the
form of a 457 deferred compensation. Although there
are differences between these plans, the commonality is
that this is very likely a significant chunk of your
retirement savings. Another important consideration is
that your 401(k) is most likely a large chunk of money
that you've never paid taxes on.

With a strong 401(k) portfolio, the next step is to decide
what to do with all that money that has been saved and
what the benefits are to **YOU**. A few of these topics

which will be discussed more fully throughout the book are:

- The IRA Discussion: A big benefit of rolling over your 401(k) into an IRA is that you typically get more investment options. If you contribute to your employer's retirement plan, you might end up with only a few investment options. You might have to be heavily invested in company stock or might have a limited number of high cost mutual funds to choose from. You also might end up with having one stable value option, which is a fixed rate, which becomes more and more appealing, and more and more appropriate as you approach retirement, but at a potentially less than desirable rate of return.

- Instead of relying on these investment options, some of which you might not be comfortable with, you can roll your plan over to an IRA and have nearly the entire universe of options available to you.

- Fees can also play a role in a 401(k) rollover. Fees in a 401(k) might be less than they are in an IRA, or the fees in a 401(k) might be more than they are in an IRA.

- Rolling over a 401(k) can also help decrease or even eliminate risk. What if you don't want all of your money invested into traditional market investments that you might feel are too risky and too up and down? By rolling your money out of an employer-sponsored plan, you gain flexibility and control, and it prevents being overly exposed to market risk at a period of time when you probably shouldn't be, or maybe don't want to be. If you desire something that has no risk of loss, you're probably going to need to give up upside potential, or you might be tying that money up for a period of time.

The most important thing to remember is that no matter what decision you make, a successful financial future starts with a plan. Whether you roll money out of your plan or leave it where it is, the topics discussed in *The Ultimate 401(k) Plan* should allow you to move forward, excited about what lies ahead and confident that your plan will work as hard for you as you have to get here. You will move forward in confidence, knowing that you've addressed all the options and have selected the best plan for you and your family's financial future.

CHAPTER ONE

Why *SHOULD* You Rollover Your 401(k)?

"Planning is bringing the future into the present, so that you can do something about it now."

Alan Lakein

In order to maximize the amount of money you have

available for your impending retirement, an important

strategy to consider is the 401(k) rollover. You might

be asking yourself why you should consider rolling

over your 401(k), or other employer-sponsored plan?

There are several important reasons why this *should* be

an important consideration for your financial future.

Reason #1: Control

The reality of your 401(k) plan is that there are a limited

number of investment options available to you that you

can choose from within that plan. Many of these

investment options are designed for long-term growth

and accumulation; both sound good, but are best

accomplished when you are (1) consistently depositing

money and (2) never drawing money out. In my experience with the clients I have worked with over the years, we have found that a lot of these plan choices rely more and more on target-date funds, allowing you, the investor, less and less opportunity to diversify when looking not just at that plan, but at your full financial picture (which most likely involves multiple buckets of money).

ULTIMATE FACT: Mutual funds are not taxed like stocks. They are taxed based on the way the fund manager trades the securities within the fund. (3)

A limitation of the 401(k) is that you have to choose from a pre-selected list of options. The reality of that list is that it is typically made up of mutual fund options. Perhaps one company stock and one stable value fund, but for those of you familiar with these stable value funds, currently they are paying a lot less interest than they used to.

ULTIMATE FACT: A Stable Value Fund is an investment vehicle found in company retirement plans. Stable value funds are comprised of mostly synthetic guaranteed investment certificates (GICs), also known as wrapped bonds, because of their inherent stability. These bonds can be short or intermediate term with longer maturities than other choices such as money market funds. They are paired, or wrapped, with insurance contracts to guarantee a specific minimum return. (4)

Therefore, the flexibility of rolling your money out of an employer-sponsored plan and into an IRA allows you to choose from not just mutual funds, stocks or fixed account options. You now have the ability to look at a number of guaranteed products or alternative products, and it opens up the opportunity to invest in many, many more things, giving you added *control*

and *flexibility* of your financial future.

Reason #2: Ability to withdraw

Another consideration for rolling over your 401(k) are

withdrawals. Where rollovers into traditional IRA

plans are 100% tax-free, it is important to realize that

withdrawals are **NOT** rollovers. On rollovers there is

no tax withholding, but if you draw money out of a

401(k) to take it as a distribution, you will automatically

be withheld a 20 percent federal tax. This might be a

deterrent for you in looking at your larger financial

picture when deciding how best to optimize your

savings.

You also might already be paying ample taxes from another source, or you might decide that you wish to withhold more than the required amount. Your ability to control the taxation, or should I say the *tax withholding* on those withdrawals, can end up being an important consideration.

> ULTIMATE FACT: 20% of Americans tap into their 401(k) assets early, either through a loan or withdrawal.   (5)

Reason #3: Required minimum distribution

Another factor to consider with a 401(k) rollover is the *required minimum distribution*.

Unfortunately, you cannot keep retirement funds in your account forever. You are forced to start taking withdrawals from your IRA, SIMPLE IRA, SEP IRA, or other retirement plan account when you reach age 70½.

Your **required minimum distribution** is the minimum amount you must withdraw from your account each year. The only exception is a ROTH IRA, which does not require withdrawals until after the death of the owner of the account. With a required minimum distribution:

- You can withdraw more than the minimum required amount.

- Your withdrawals will be included in your taxable income, except for any part that was taxed before (your basis) or that can be received tax-free (such as qualified distributions from designated ROTH accounts).

While you can select which IRA plans to withdraw your RMD from (valuable if you have some plans that are performing better than others), you do NOT have this ability with an employer-sponsored plan. If you have left retirement monies in the employer plan and have since left that employer, you will be FORCED to process an RMD out of that specific account every year starting at age 70 ½.

Reason #4: The ROTH IRA Opportunity

Another benefit of rolling the money out of the 401(k) and getting that money into an IRA is that it allows you the opportunity to address the ROTH IRA conversion strategy. Of course, with a traditional IRA or a traditional 401(k), every dollar you take out will be taxed as ordinary income.

However, when looking at a ROTH IRA, they grow tax-deferred **and** tax-free forever AND there is no required minimum distribution at age 70 ½. Every dollar that you make grows tax-free, so whenever you take that money out, there are *no taxes on it whatsoever.* When you pass away, that money can continue to go tax-free to the beneficiary, so it continues to grow tax-free. This is a fantastic opportunity when we take into consideration the current taxes relative to where tax rates could potentially go in the future.

In Summary:

Being able to control exactly how you want your money invested, what the tax withholding of withdrawals is going to be *and* having an opportunity to address the ROTH conversion opportunity are some of the primary benefits of rolling money out of an

employer-sponsored 401(k) plan.

(6)

ROTH Conversion Calculator

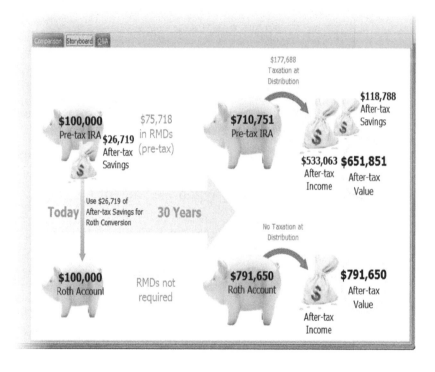

Another consideration is, of course, how this decision

fits in with your full financial picture. The limitation of

a 401(k) is that it's looking at one account, when in

reality, you most likely have multiple accounts to consider in your overall retirement plan. Opportunities in an IRA might allow you to better diversify the overall strategy more than the limitations of 401(k) investments.

CHAPTER 2

Why *SHOULDN'T* You Roll Money out of Your 401(k)?

"A goal without a plan is just a wish."

Antoine de Saint-Exupery

Though there are many benefits to rolling money out of your employer-sponsored plan into an IRA, there are also considerations that make it more advantageous for you to NOT rollover your 401(k).

Consideration #1: Retirement Age

One important thing to think about when deciding what action to take with your 401(k) plan is when you plan to retire. If you are going to retire before 59 ½, there are ways to access money out of your 401(k) after the age of 55, yet before the age of 59 ½, that you do not have in a traditional IRA.

You do have the ability to draw money out of an IRA prior to age 59 ½ *if* taken in a very specific way, known as a "72(t) withdrawal". The reality is that you most likely would not want to do either of these types of withdrawals, but taking money out of a 401(k) prior to 59 ½, yet after 55, can be a little bit easier than drawing it out of an IRA.

Now what if you're on the other end of the spectrum and you plan to work past the age of 70 ½? In this case, the earliest you would typically draw money out of your employer-sponsored plan is age 59 ½. At age 70 ½, you are forced to draw money out of your retirement plan, with the exception of the employer-sponsored plan where you are presently working.

If you plan to work beyond age 70 ½ and you have 401(k) monies in that plan, you are not forced to take a required minimum distribution out of your plan. Mind you, if you have other retirement plans not with your employer and you're past 70 ½, you do have to take money out of those plans. Whether you plan to retire early or have plans for a long work-life, your 401(k) is impacted in different ways.

Consideration #2: Company Stock

Many people may or may not be aware that they have company stock in their 401(k). Now if your company stock has gone down, this is less of a consideration when making your decision. However, if your company stock has gone up significantly, you might have the opportunity to take advantage of something known as a "net unrealized appreciation." The short version of this is that it will allow you, if done correctly, to draw that stock out, paying ordinary income tax on the original basis it was purchased for, and paying capital gains tax rates on any gains. This can be a huge opportunity that many people might not be aware of.

Now for the catch: This opportunity might force you to take out all of the money in your 401(k). Keep in mind, you're not taxed on all the money – only the basis of the stock- but it can be a huge opportunity and tax savings for people that hold a lot of highly-appreciated company stock.

Consideration #3: Stable Value Fund

Another consideration is your **stable value fund**. I talk about this type of fund often with my clients. Consider this scenario that I often encounter: You find yourself approaching retirement. Naturally you're feeling less and less comfortable with risk, so you prefer to take less and less risk in your 401(k) investments. Perhaps you're not moving into bonds, so you find yourself investing in stable value funds.

ULTIMATE FACT: In times of economic recession or stock market volatility, stable value funds can be one of the most valuable investments. While many other investment returns are much lower in hard times, stable value funds remain just that, stable. The owner of the investment continues to receive the agreed-upon interest rate and the full principal regardless of the state of the economy. (7)

As I mentioned earlier, these rates have typically dropped significantly from what they once were, but if you move money out of your employer-sponsored plan, you lose access to that employer-sponsored stable value fund.

There are other investment options available and not to say that you can't do better than that rate; maybe you can and maybe you can't. But if you want something that is almost a liquid fixed account, your 401(k) might offer you a higher rate than the similar investment outside of it.

Consideration #4: Does your employer match?

Another key consideration is the company match to your 401(k) contribution. In rolling money out of your 401(k) into a traditional IRA, you DO NOT lose any of the matched contributions that you have already received. If you plan on taking advantage of your company's in-service withdrawal provision (i.e. your ability to roll assets into your IRA while continuing to work) your 401(k) will remain open to ongoing contributions and your future contributions will

continue to be matched.

Why Your 401(k) Contribution Matters

People are living longer:

HEALTHY
65-YEAR-OLD
COUPLE:

50% chance
at least one
will live to age 92 ½

Source: Annuity 2000 Mortality Table, Society of Actuaries. Figures assume a person is in good health.

(8)

If you're still working at the company with your

sponsored 401(k) plan, and you're planning to roll your

money over, you are not losing anything and ongoing

contributions continue to be matched. There is not a

negative impact from a match perspective; you're

simply moving some of the money off of the table to

secure it in a different place rather than leaving it all in one place.

CHAPTER 3

TAXES

"You must pay taxes,
but there's no law that says you gotta leave a tip"

Morgan Stanley Advertisement

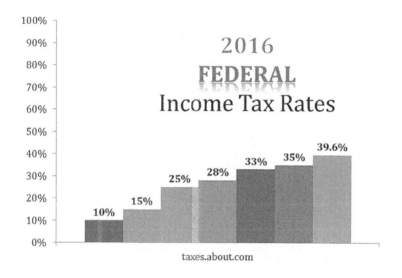

(9)

As much time as people dedicate to trying to get a

better rate of return on their investments, too often

taxes end up being a neglected, though hugely

important subject. Most people feel they certainly pay

their fair share of taxes, if not more than fair, yet are

typically left unaware of the tax-saving strategies

available to them. From a tax perspective, there are as

many pros and cons of rolling money out of your

401(k) into an IRA, as there are many pros and cons of

NOT rolling those same monies over.

ULTIMATE FACT: As much as 70% of your hard-earned retirement funds can be eaten up by income, estate and state taxes.   (10)

Consider this scenario: In looking at your 401(k), you

plan to not touch that money until age 59 ½. Now,

should you leave money in the 401(k) and decide to

retire before 59 ½ (yet after age 55), know that there are

special provisions that may allow you to withdraw

money out of this plan if need be. For most people,

though, 59 ½ is the earliest you can anticipate drawing

money out of the plan without incurring significant tax

penalties.

Consider a different scenario: You don't take money out of the plan, nor do you decide to roll the money over into an IRA. You find yourself at age 70 ½, the required minimum distribution age, and you still have money in an employer plan where you no longer work. Because of this, you will be forced to take a required minimum distribution out of that account, and *you will be forced to withhold 20 percent in federal taxes.* Your first required minimum distribution is due by April 1 of the year after you turn 70 ½. Your second and all subsequent distributions must be taken by December 31 each year. If you delay your first distribution until April, you are required to take two distributions in the same year, which could result in an unusually high tax bill or even bump you into a higher tax bracket. In certain unique instances, taking two withdrawals in one year may be advantageous, but the vast majority of the time you will want to avoid doing this, as you will be significantly increasing your taxable income.

If your significantly younger spouse will inherit your IRA, you may be able to reduce your required distributions, thereby trimming taxes and making your retirement funds last longer. RMDs are calculated using factors that include your life expectancy as determined by the IRS. If you've named a spouse as the sole beneficiary of your IRA, and he or she is at least 10 years younger than you, then your RMD is computed using a joint-life expectancy table. That will reduce the amount you need to distribute in any given year.

For example, a retiree who turned 70 ½ in the previous year and who would have to take his first RMD by April 1 of the current year, would have a life expectancy of 27.4 years in the eyes of the IRS. So if his IRA was worth $200,000, his first RMD would be $7,547 ($200,000 divided by 26.5). But let's say he designates his 56-year-old wife to be the sole beneficiary of that retirement account. In that case, their joint life expectancy would be 30.1 years. So the first RMD would be trimmed to $6,645.

While everyone's situation is unique, the reason you would not want to put yourself in the scenario above is that you have the flexibility with IRAs (Individual Retirement Accounts), which is where you'd be rolling a 401(k) plan or a 403(b) plan over to. In this scenario, you have the ability to pick and choose which accounts to take your required minimum distribution from. You can take it over a period of time. You can take it all at once. Most importantly, you will gain the ability to take

RMD withdrawals from certain accounts while leaving other accounts untouched, therefore making it much easier to effectively design a life-long laddered income strategy, utilizing the benefits of multiple buckets.

Taking an approach such as the one mentioned above puts the *CONTROL* back into your hands. When leaving money in an old employer-sponsored plan, you lose a lot of flexibility. You have to draw that money out and they're going to force you to take at least 20 percent federal tax withholding from it. Maybe that's what you owe. Maybe it's not. But, you are not entitled to make that decision and it could end up costing you down the road. *Rolling your money over into an IRA provides so much more flexibility, not just in terms of investment options, but also in your increased ability to manage taxes.*

Another important consideration is that you can roll money out of a 401(k) into an IRA and as we know, convert that money into a ROTH. There is a long list of factors and considerations before doing this, but one of the primary factors is *TIME*. If we have a sum of money that's invested, the long-term goal for that money is for it to continue to grow.

If you look 5 years from now, 10 years from now, even 15 years from now, do you feel taxes are going to be higher or lower than they presently are? In all likelihood you might find yourself in a higher tax situation. Note that this might not be a result of you having higher income, just higher tax rates. Imagine if you could convert this pre-tax money (which is going to increase your future tax liability) to after-tax money to tax-free money in a ROTH, that would grow tax-free forever, that is not forced to take a required minimum distribution at age 70 ½, and that could pass to your spouse or your heirs 100 percent tax-free from taxable income. What a powerful opportunity!

If you worked for an employer for a long period of time, perhaps over ten years, you may have found yourself putting after-tax money into your 401(k), or you might actually have ROTH monies already contributed into the plan.

Converting traditional 401(k)s, pre-tax monies into an IRA, rolling them into an IRA and then converting them to a ROTH is much like just converting an IRA to a ROTH – a taxable event with 100 percent of those monies taxed as ordinary income in that calendar year.

If you have after-tax money in your 401(k), that money can be moved out of the 401(k) upon rollover with no tax impact and typically no fee. Then you can take that money and go directly into a ROTH IRA **without** paying any taxes on it! This option allows you to potentially take a large sum of money and shift it into a tax-free account as an opportunity that you very well might not have otherwise.

Furthering the conversation on flexibility, this allows you yet another bucket that not only are you not forced to take a required minimum distribution from, but the growth is tax-free as long as you leave it there. When talking about different buckets of money, if you have one that is going to grow tax-free forever, you need to ask yourself when you would want to draw that money out? Probably as late as possible; possibly never.

When we think about our 401(k), we've saved all this money up, but after taxes how much money is that really? People typically don't anticipate taking that money out all at once, but what if there was a need to do so? Or what is the cost if we decide that we wish to keep the money as is? There is a cost to that and the cost is you might leave it in liquid cash not making a whole heck of a lot, or you leave it in the market and you find yourself taking more risk than you really should be or more importantly, are comfortable taking.

Obviously everyone's risk tolerance is different, but there is a critical transition that takes place from saving into a retirement plan and letting that grow, versus the fact that you are retired and a constant paycheck is no longer coming in. You find yourself drawing on your investments and looking to make every dollar count, so tax decisions become hugely important.

You need to make sure before making any of these types of decisions that you are looking very closely at your tax return and getting professional advice; I cannot emphasize enough the importance of factoring in those taxes with every decision you are making in regards to your retirement money.

CHAPTER 4

Pensions

*"Most people don't plan to fail,
they fail to plan."*

John Beckley

It's time to retire. **Congratulations – you've made it!** You've worked for an employer that not only offered you a 401(k), but a pension plan as well. Your company notified you that you have the option of taking the pension as a lump sum, or as a payment for the rest of your life (and perhaps your life and the life of someone else). **WHAT DO YOU DO?**

*For the purpose of this discussion, let's use a real life client example: We'll refer to them as Mr. and Mrs. Smith. Mrs. Smith worked for an employer that offered her the option of a lump sum pension benefit OR a lifetime payment. At the time of her retirement, she had available a $620,000 lump sum to be taken all at once **OR** an annual payment of $42,000 a year, every year, for the rest of her and her husband's lives. What should she do?!*

Option #1: Taking your maximum benefit vs. a lesser benefit

When faced with the huge, once in a lifetime decision of a pension election, there are many different factors to consider. Do you take a maximum benefit and say "Instead of the $42,000 a year we'll take $50,000 a year"? (factoring in the money given to you to guarantee income for a second life). Though the clear benefit here is a much larger annual income for the rest of Mrs. Smith's life, the concern and risk is that Mrs. Smith will die first and that the monthly income will stop AND there will be no lump sum amount left for Mr. Smith or their family.

OR do you take a lesser benefit? Instead of that $50,000 per year, they decide to forego $8,000 a year. They decide to take $42,000 a year and have that pay out for the rest of both of their lives. Once the second spouse passes, the money is gone. In this 'once in a lifetime decision' that you have to make, what are you to do? Obviously, as with most situations in financial planning, everyone's situation is different and there are a lot of variables to be weighed.

There are pros and cons to each scenario. Should you elect to take that lump sum benefit and roll the money over into your IRA, there are no taxes in doing so. You now have full control of that money. This control can have both positive and negative effects. Should you make the wrong decision investment-wise at that time, you could lose a lot of that money and never make it back. Should you take that money and roll it into the bank at current interest rates, the benefit is that it is secure (the negative is that it is potentially not earning enough interest to keep up with your income needs nor inflation).

Certainly the goal, whichever option you elect, is to provide as much income as possible for the rest of your lives. In addition, ideally, should you not spend all the money, you will have some type of a remainder interest left after your spouse passes, which can then go towards family, schools, churches or whatever institutions or people are important to you.

Option #2: Taking a lump sum pension

Let's get back to our 'once in a lifetime' decision. Should you decide to take the pension as a lump sum and roll it into an IRA, that is now your money that you have full, 100% control over. You're now faced with the decision of how best to allocate and invest that money based on your needs and comfort level with various investments. Almost all the time, it is wisest to invest in more than one type of investment. We've heard the advice before and often the best advice is the simplest: "Don't put all of your eggs in one basket" certainly tends to make sense here. So what types of different buckets exist? It is desirable to have one bucket for growth, one bucket for liquidity and one bucket for safety.

All pensions are not created equal

Different employers-and this is a key thing to factor in - have different pensions that pay out different amounts. Unfortunately, depending on the employer's plan, you are dealing with entirely different numbers and percentages; this adds complexity to an already difficult decision. There is a myriad of different factors that can adjust how much your employer will pay you out, but it comes down to that core goal of **control**. Do you take the lump sum and control the investment of that money, or do you take it as a payout and ensure that you're going to get this income for the rest of your life?

In looking at your employer and their pension plan, some employers do not offer lump sum amounts; your only option is to trigger a lifetime benefit. You may have heard of a related subject involving a *pension max decision*. What that means comes back to our original example.

Instead of $50,000 year, we'll give you $42,000 a year to guarantee an income for that second life. Of course the only reason you take $8,000 less a year is to ensure that income is going to be paid out for two lives as opposed to one.

Life Insurance

Now comes a conversation about life insurance. The difference between the $50,000 and the $42,000 payout is $8,000 a year. Could you buy life insurance on the owner of that primary annuitant, the pensioner, for less than that $8,000 a year that would provide the same $42,000 annual income for a beneficiary? Sometimes yes. Sometimes no.

This is a strategy that you should address and a decision that you have to make **before** the election of the pension. You certainly don't want to make a decision based on getting life insurance, only to find out that you will not be issued the policy as applied for, or maybe not at all. Now you've made an irreversible election and put yourself in a dangerous position.

ULTIMATE FACT: A Pension Max Decision is a cash flow analysis that is used to determine whether a retiree's pension dollars can be stretched further with the purchase of a life insurance policy. (11)

You also need to consider when to start your pension benefit, because if you defer, perhaps your future benefit amount will continue to grow. When to start a pension, how to draw that pension, and IF to draw a pension at all are crucial decisions that all too often are not given the adequate time and consideration they need to ensure that you truly maximize your family's retirement.

Conclusion

"There is only one success,
to be able to spend your life in your own way."

Christopher Morley

The best advice is often simple and short; what so much of this comes down to is the number one concern that people have in regards to retirement today.

Is it enough? More specifically, is what we've saved enough to last the rest of our lives?

What people are asking is: *What type of income can we sustainably generate off the money that we've saved, and what are the risks of that not working out?* As much as financial plans can be designed and algorithms can be run and all types of analyses can be put together (which all can potentially add value), perhaps the most valuable thing would be to look at it as simply as possible.

You need three buckets of money in retirement.

Bucket Number 1: Monthly Expenses

This bucket is the amount of money that you're pretty certain you'll spend every month. This is where it is critical to do a budget to determine what your typical costs are on a monthly basis. These will be fixed costs like property taxes, car payments, or the electrical bill as well as variable costs such as going out to dinner. You don't work and save money diligently for decades so that you can retire and no longer be able to live the life you want. Just as everyone's life and lifestyle is different, people will have drastically different numbers for Bucket Number 1.

The goal is to have enough money coming in to pay your expenses while making sure you don't have TOO much coming in. Sounds funny doesn't it? Often when asked the question of "Do you need more income?"

clients respond, "Who wouldn't want more income?".

Financial planning is about strategy and not just how much income do we need, but also where's the best place to draw that income from? You don't want to draw out more income than you will spend, because you will most likely be withdrawing that money from accounts at higher, tax-advantaged growth rates than the annually taxable, low interest rate bank account that you will let unspent money accumulate in.

Thus, regardless of the amount, Bucket 1 is a number that you're fairly confident you will spend every month.

Bucket Number 2: Readily Available Cash Liquidity

The second bucket needs to provide liquidity for things like going on a vacation, buying a car, helping out family, or fixing a roof. While these are not monthly "must-haves," we all know that things will come up and having short-term funds available to cover those costs prevents us from having to draw monies from Bucket Number 3 and potentially negatively impact our longer-term growth money.

Bucket Number 3: Long-Term Protection

This important bucket takes into account our ever-increasing life expectancy as a result of ever- advancing medical care and healthcare systems. People are living longer and longer, and you need your money to carry you through. Regardless of your savings amount, you need to ensure that you're accounting for some type of future growth. As much as we need monthly cash flow and emergency funds available, we also need to be aware that everything we spend money on today will increase in cost over time and we need to have a future growth strategy in place to ensure that we can keep up with those costs.

So do you have enough income to last the rest of your life?

The Steps Towards Gaining Retirement Confidence

One of the first things to look at would be a budget to identify how much money you spend every month. How you begin to do this is to write down everything you spend money on in a month. It sounds very simple, and it is very simple. Be honest about it. The more detailed that budget is, the more likely it is to be accurate.

The goal, of course, is to pay taxes only on the monies

that you anticipate spending. We go through a budget

to identify what your first chunk of income needs to be.

Then we determine what the true liquidity need is;

emergency money, cash on hand to gain access to, etc.

It might not be sitting in the bank, perhaps it's a

brokerage account or even a retirement account, but

something that you could get access to very quickly.

A lot of times when we're talking about 401(k)s, we're

talking about Bucket Number 3. You can see how we

often find ourselves in a conversation about ROTH

conversions. If you could have your money grow, only

to pay even more taxes on that growth in the future or

to grow entirely tax free forever, which would you

choose? Perhaps this sounds overly simplified but

we've all heard the phrase that "It's not about what you make, it's about what you keep". ROTH IRAs allow the owner to keep 100% of their money and this is obviously VERY attractive.

Managing a portfolio for growth is very different from managing a portfolio for current income. While one strategy involves constant saving, long time deferral, and no withdrawals the latter involves constant withdrawals, laddered time strategies, and no saving. Different tools and investments exist for different purposes. The limitation of the 401(k) is that typically the investments available in these plans are designed for *long-term accumulation*. We add money consistently every time we get paid. We're not trying to time the market; we're trying to save as much as we can. We're not thinking a lot about "up days" and "down days," we're thinking about a consistent, steady strategy of long-term savings.

What is also taken into consideration is that in all likelihood you didn't take any money out of your 401(k). So now you have 20, 30, perhaps even 40 years of ongoing contributions into a market-based account that has grown in value. The reality of that is, even if you think of the most recent decade whenever you're reading this book, instead of adding into that account, what if you were steadily drawing money out of the account every month? What would your account value look like at the end of that decade? The result would look drastically different from what it presently does.

Timing of Withdrawals

(12)

Age	Mr. Smith Investment: $100,000 Stocks 60% | Bonds 40% Retired 1/1/1969 – Annual withdrawals: $5,000			Ms. Jones Investment: $100,000 Stocks 60% | Bonds 40% Retired 1/1/1979 – Annual withdrawals: $5,000		
	Year	ROR	Year-end value	Year	ROR	Year-end value
65	1969	-2.6%	$92,168	1979	14.7%	$109,172
66	1970	5.3%	$91,449	1980	23.9%	$128,899
67	1971	10.5%	$95,219	1981	3.4%	$126,282
68	1972	12.9%	$101,447	1982	16.6%	$139,848
69	1973	-6.6%	$88,410	1983	16.6%	$155,426
70	1974	-12.6%	$70,219	1984	7.3%	$158,880
71	1975	25.1%	$80,085	1985	22.0%	$185,630
72	1976	16.5%	$85,107	1986	13.9%	$203,223
73	1977	-2.4%	$74,324	1987	5.7%	$206,232
74	1978	6.3%	$69,660	1988	12.2%	$222,537
75	1979	14.7%	$69,487	1989	22.1%	$262,402
76	1980	23.9%	$74,222	1990	1.2%	$255,753
77	1981	3.4%	$63,670	1991	20.8%	$298,808
78	1982	16.6%	$60,391	1992	6.1%	$306,574
79	1983	16.6%	$56,145	1993	7.3%	$318,026
80	1984	7.3%	$45,480	1994	2.0%	$313,351
81	1985	22.0%	$40,198	1995	24.6%	$378,884
82	1986	13.9%	$30,286	1996	16.3%	$429,072
83	1987	5.7%	$15,941	1997	21.1%	$507,502
84	1988	12.2%	$1,176	1998	19.1%	$592,094
85	1989	22.1%	Exhausted	1999	14.3%	$664,249
86	1990	1.2%	Exhausted	2000	-0.8%	$645,969
87	1991	20.8%	Exhausted	2001	-3.8%	$608,120
88	1992	6.1%	Exhausted	2002	-9.3%	$538,413
89	1993	7.3%	Exhausted	2003	18.9%	$626,319
90	1994	2.0%	Exhausted	2004	8.2%	$663,790
91	1995	24.6%	Exhausted	2005	3.8%	$674,761
92	1996	16.3%	Exhausted	2006	11.2%	$735,149
93	1997	21.1%	Exhausted	2007	6.1%	$764,278
94	1998	19.1%	Exhausted	2008	-20.5%	$591,402

Mr. Smith — Average ROR 10.5%

Ms. Jones — Average ROR 9.6%

Putting It All Together

So: *"Did you save enough money for retirement?"* It's not

about trying to double your money as quickly as

possible. It's about developing a strategy and having a

plan that takes into consideration what you have saved

and what you require that money to do for you. It's

about designing a realistic retirement income plan so

that you can enjoy doing all the things you hoped

you'd be doing, without the stress of feeling like you're

going to run out of money. It's creating a budget that

will help you to ensure you're not paying taxes on

monies that you don't yet need to be paying taxes on;

money that will better serve you growing for when

you'll need it. We know the rules of investing. We

know that you don't put all your eggs in one basket.

We know that the market will go up and down. Typical

investing theory says you don't sell down, you hold on and it will come back. Few doubt that coming back is in fact what will occur; the concern of course, is how long will you have to wait?

As you get older, in all likelihood you will want your total market risk to decrease. As we consider all these things and consider how long you plan to work, when you anticipate triggering an income and how long you need that income to last, we begin to understand what makes the most sense in your specific situation. It is this process of addressing the many facets of your financial life and developing a sound plan that will best help you to eliminate the concerns and fears too often associated with retiring. As we hope for the best-case scenario, we need to plan for the worst case to ensure that retirement will be everything you hoped it would be.

REFERENCES

1 Kirkham, Elyssa. (2015, October, 5). 62% of Americans Have Under $1,000 in Savings, Survey Says. Retrieved from https://www.gobankingrates.com/savings-account/62-percent-americans-under-1000-savings-survey-finds/

2 Collinson, Catherine (2015, December). The Current State of Retirement: Pre-Retiree Expectations and Retiree Realities. Retrieved from https://www.transamericacenter.org/docs/default-source/retirees-survey/retirees_survey_2015_report.pdf

3 Campbell, Kelly. (2011, February 16). 5 Things Investors Should Know About Mutual Funds. Retrieved from http://money.usnews.com/money/blogs/the-smarter-mutual-fund-investor/2011/02/16/5-things-investors-should-know-about-mutual-funds

4 Stable Value Investment Association. (2013). Stable Value FAQ. Retrieved from http://stablevalue.org/media/misc/Stable_Value_FAQ.pdf

5 Frankel, Matthew. (2016, January26). 20 Retirement Stats That Will Blow You Away. Retrieved from http://www.fool.com/retirement/general/2016/01/26/20-retirement-stats-that-will-blow-you-away.aspx

6 Trust Builders, Inc. (2016) Roth Conversion Calculator. Retrieved from http://www.asktrak.com/calculators/roth-conversion/

7 Investopedia, LLC. (2017) Stable Value Fund. Retrieved from http://www.investopedia.com/terms/s/stable-value-fund.asp

8 PIMCO. (2017). Talk About Retirement. Retrieved from https://www.pimco.com/resources/smartcharts/topics-to-talk-about/talk-about-retirement

REFERENCES

9 Perez, William. (2017, January 27). Federal Income Tax Rates for the Year 2016. Retrieved from https://www.thebalance.com/federal-income-tax-rates-for-the-year-2016-3193200

10 Haggin Geary, Leslie. (2017). 9 savvy ways to withdraw retirement funds. Retrieved from http://www.bankrate.com/finance/retirement/ways-to-withdraw-retirement-funds-1.aspx

11 Garland, Susan. (2013, September). A Pension Strategy That Could Backfire. Retrieved from http://www.kiplinger.com/article/retirement/T037-C000-S004-a-pension-strategy-that-could-backfire.html

12 John Hancock. (2015). Sequence of Returns. Retrieved from http://www.jhrollover.com/gifl/sequence_of_returns.html

GLOSSARY OF TERMS

72(t) Withdrawal - Rule 72(t), issued by the Internal Revenue Service (IRS), permits penalty-free withdrawals from IRA accounts, provided the owner takes at least five substantially equal periodic payments (SEPPs), with the amount depending on the owner's life expectancy as calculated through IRS-approved methods.

401(k) – **A** 401(k) Plan is a **defined** contribution plan where an employee can make contributions from his or her paycheck either before or after-tax, depending on the options offered in the plan. The contributions go into a 401(k) account, with the employee often choosing the investments based on options provided under the plan.

403(b) - A 403(b) plan, also known as a tax-sheltered annuity (TSA) plan, is a retirement plan for certain employees of public schools, employees of certain tax-exempt organizations, and certain ministers.

457 Plan - The 457 plan is a type of nonqualified, tax advantaged deferred-compensation retirement plan that is available for governmental and certain non-governmental employers in the United States. The employer provides the plan and the employee defers compensation into it on a pre-tax basis.

Mutual Fund - An investment program funded by shareholders that trades in diversified holdings and is professionally managed.

Net Unrealized Appreciation - The cost basis is the average of the individual values of employer stock when each portion was contributed to the plan or purchased by the plan's trustee. The difference between the cost basis and the market value at the time of distribution is called the net unrealized appreciation (or "NUA").

Required Minimum Distribution - A required minimum distribution is the amount the federal government requires you to withdraw each year – usually after you reach age 70½ – from retirement accounts, including traditional IRAs, simplified employee pension (SEP) IRAs and SIMPLE IRAs, as well as many employer-sponsored retirement plans.

The RMD is designed to ensure that you withdraw at least a portion of the funds in your account over your lifetime – and that you pay taxes on those funds. Withdrawing less than the required minimum will result in a potentially hefty penalty: The amount not withdrawn is taxed at 50%.

ROTH IRA - An individual retirement account allowing a person to set aside after-tax income up to a specified amount each year. Both earnings on the account and withdrawals after age 59½ are tax-free.

SEP IRA - A SEP IRA is a type of traditional IRA for self-employed individuals or small business owners.

(SEP stands for Simplified Employee Pension.) Any business owner with one or more employees, or anyone with freelance income, can open a SEP IRA.

Simple IRA - A SIMPLE IRA is a retirement plan that may be established by employers, including self-employed individuals (sole proprietorships and partnerships). The SIMPLE IRA allows eligible employees to contribute part of their pretax compensation to the plan. This means the tax on the money is deferred until it is distributed.

Stable Value Fund - A stable value fund is an investment vehicle found in company retirement plans. Stable value funds are comprised of mostly synthetic guaranteed investment certificates (GICs), also known as wrapped bonds, because of their inherent stability. These bonds can be short or intermediate term with longer maturities than other choices such as money market funds. They are paired, or wrapped, with insurance contracts to guarantee a specific minimum return.

Target-Date Fund - Also known as a lifecycle, dynamic-risk or age-based fund – is a collective investment scheme, often a mutual fund or a collective trust fund, designed to provide a simple investment solution through a portfolio whose asset allocation mix becomes more conservative as the target date (usually retirement) approaches.

Made in the USA
Coppell, TX
08 March 2022

74649724R00044